## DATE DUE

|  |  |  |  |
|--|--|--|--|
|  |  |  |  |
|  |  |  |  |
|  |  |  |  |
|  |  |  |  |
|  |  |  |  |
|  |  |  |  |
|  |  |  |  |
|  |  |  |  |
|  |  |  |  |
|  |  |  |  |
|  |  |  |  |
|  |  |  |  |
|  |  |  |  |
|  |  |  |  |

952
REY        Reynolds, Jeff
c.l        Japan

BC#34880000074067  $16.95

*Morrill Elementary School*
*Chicago Public Schools*
*6011 South Rockwell Street*
*Chicago, IL 60629*

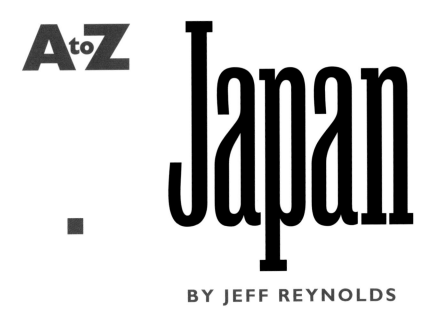

# A to Z

# Japan

## BY JEFF REYNOLDS

children's press®

A Division of Scholastic Inc.
New York Toronto London Auckland Sydney
Mexico City New Delhi Hong Kong
Danbury, Connecticut

Consultant: Susanna Hapgood, Research Associate, University of Michigan
Series Design: Marie O'Neill
Photo Research: Candlepants Incorporated

*For Linda Cornwell – J.R.*

The photos on the cover show Japanese snow monkeys (top left), a close-up view of the Heian-Jingu Shrine (top right), a cherry tree branch with blossoms (bottom right), and a girl in traditional Japanese dress (center).

Photographs © 2004: Corbis Images: 25 bottom (B.S.P.I.), 13, 32 (Bettmann), 4 top (Tom Brakefield), 15, 17 left (Christie's Images), 27 left (Ric Ergenbright), 14 (Historical Picture Archive), 8 (Japack Company), 5 top (Steve Kaufman), 9 top left (Bob Krist), 6 top (Craig Lovell), 7 (Jose Fuste Raga), 29 (Chris Rainier), 23 left (Royalty-Free), 6 bottom, 16 top, 22, 23 right, 34 top (Michael S. Yamashita); Corbis SABA/Tom Wagner: 16 bottom, 26; Envision Stock Photography Inc./Steven Mark Needham: cover bottom; Getty Images: 12 top (Fox Photos), 12 bottom (Issei Kato/AFP), 33 (Toshifumi Kitamura/AFP), 28 bottom (Kazuhiro Nogi/AFP), 31 (Toru Yamanaka/AFP); Index Stock Imagery/Joe Carini: 35 bottom; Photo Researchers, NY/Porterfield/Chickering: 5 bottom; PhotoDisc/Getty Images: 27 right (John Dakers/Life File), 17 right (Akira Kaede); PictureQuest: 4 bottom, cover top left (Creatas), 34 bottom (Stockbyte); Stone/Getty Images: 25 top, 35 top (Paul Chesley), 10 left (Chad Ehlers), 9 top right, 28 top (Charles Gupton), cover top right (Will & Deni McIntyre), 18, 19, 38 (Orion Press); Superstock, Inc.: 9 bottom (George Hunter), 30 (Ben Mangor), cover center (Steve Vidler), 24 left; Taxi/Getty Images/Diane Padys: 11; The Image Bank/Getty Images/Kaz Chiba: 24 top; The Image Works: 10 right, 34 center, 37 top (Fujifotos), 36 top (Mitsuru Kanamori/HAGA), 36 bottom (Takashi Kihara/HAGA), 37 bottom (Toshiro Morita/HAGA).
Map by XNR Productions, Inc.

Library of Congress Cataloging-in-Publication Data

Reynolds, Jeff.
  Japan / by Jeff Reynolds.
    p. cm. — (A to Z)
  Includes index.
Contents: Animals – Buildings – Cities – Dress – Exports – Food –
Government – History – Important people – Jobs – Keepsakes – Land
– Map – Nation – Only in Japan – People – Question – Religion –
School and sports – Transportation – Unusual Places – Visiting the
Country – Window to the past – X-tra special things – Yearly
festivals – Z – Let's Explore More.
ISBN 0-516-23655-5 (lib. bdg.)     0-516-25072-8 (pbk.)
  1. Japan—Juvenile literature. I. Title. II. Series.
  DS806.R369 2005
  952'.003—dc22
                          2004003288

1 2 3 4 5 6 7 8 9 10 R 13 12 11 10 09 08 07 06 05 04

# Contents

Japanese macaques are sometimes called "snow monkeys."

# Animals

Japan has many amazing animals and insects like **cicadas**, Japanese macaques, Blackiston's fish owls, and loggerhead turtles.

Cicada

There are only about 100 Blackiston's fish owls that live in the wild.

Cicadas are insects known for making loud, whirring sounds. If you live in Japan, a cicada just might be your favorite pet!

Japanese **macaques** are a type of monkey. They have thick fur that helps them to survive in cold mountainous areas. This is why they are sometimes called "snow monkeys."

Loggerhead turtles spend most of their lives in the ocean.

There are also Blackiston's fish owls. They are nighttime hunters. They live near lakes and rivers, feeding on fish. They are nearly **extinct**.

Loggerhead turtles lay their eggs on the beaches of Japan. The oldest ones grow to be very large.

**Todaiji Temple**

# Buildings

**Tokyo's City Hall**

Modern high-rise office and apartment buildings can be found in all Japanese cities. Look at the great building that is Tokyo's City Hall.

Japan is also home to ancient **temples** and **shrines**. Some of them are several centuries old. The Todaiji Temple, near the old city of Nara, is the largest wooden building in the world. It has burned down and been rebuilt more than once in its 1,200-year history.

**Tokyo was once named Edo.**

# Cities

Japan is a land of steep, forested mountains. These areas are not good for building towns. Most of Japan's cities are found in the level areas along the country's shores.

Tokyo is Japan's capital and its largest city. Nearly one out of every twelve people in Japan lives in Tokyo. It was once the largest city in the world. Other important Japanese cities are Sapporo, Yokohama, Nagoya, Osaka, Kobe, and Kyoto.

# Dress

On most days, the Japanese dress in much the same way North Americans do. However, at special occasions like weddings and festivals, women may wear **kimonos**.

## Ifuku

*(EE-foo-koo)* means clothing.

Geta are wooden sandals.

The kimonos worn by younger women tend to be more brightly colored than those worn by older women. An **obi**, which is a belt, is worn with a kimono. Women also wear **tabis** with their kimonos. Tabis are white, ankle-length socks.

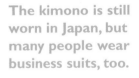

The kimono is still worn in Japan, but many people wear business suits, too.

Japanese schoolchildren wearing modern clothing

9

A car factory located near the city of Nissan

# Exports

Iron, steel, computers, cameras, and appliances are some of Japan's top exports. You probably know brand names such as Toyota, Nissan, and Mazda. These are Japanese companies that make cars.

Japanese products are prized around the world because of their high quality and low price. Japan's exports have made the country one of the world's richest nations.

Look at this human-like robot!

# Miso Soup Recipe

**WHAT YOU NEED:**
• 1 can or package of concentrated miso soup broth
**OR**
• 4 cups water
• 3 to 4 tablespoons of miso paste
• 2 cups dried bonito flakes, available in many grocery stores
• Your choice of other ingredients

**HOW TO MAKE IT:**
• Prepare broth according to the package directions or make from scratch by adding 2 cups of loose, dried bonito flakes and 3 or 4 tablespoons of miso paste to 4 cups of boiling water. Bring to a boil again. Strain the broth to remove the solids. Serve plain, or add small cubes of tofu, cooked rice or shrimp, one chopped scallion, or your favorite cooked vegetable.

# Food

Japanese children enjoy eating hamburgers, fried chicken, and other foods that are popular in North America. Rice is part of many Japanese meals, even breakfast. Soup is also a tasty part of Japanese meals. Have an adult help you prepare this recipe for **miso soup**.

Emperor Hirohito ruled Japan from 1926 to 1989.

# Government

Prime Minister
Junichiro Koizumi

Japan's government is very much like that of Great Britain. It is a **constitutional monarchy**. The emperor is more a symbol of the country than an actual ruler. Instead, a prime minister serves as the day-to-day leader of Japan's government. Junichiro Koizumi became prime minister in 2001.

Japan's government is made up of two houses of legislature: the House of Representatives and the House of Councilors. There are more than seven hundred lawmakers that make up the two houses. **Citizens** elect most of them.

The samurai wore armor that protected most of their bodies.

# History

Emperors have been in power in Japan for hundreds of years. For many centuries, though, a **shogun** was the real ruler of the country. Shogun is a word that means "highest military commander." He would give orders and say that they came from the emperor. Groups of **warriors** called **samurai** helped the shogun gain and hold onto his power. The samurai were skilled at fighting on horseback with bows and lances. Most of all, they are remembered for the swords they made and used.

13

Katsushita Hokusai created woodblock prints.

# Important People

Most Japanese paintings used to be of people and battle scenes. Two artists changed that. They made pictures of the beautiful Japanese landscape.

*Swimming Carp* is from the famous *Fish Series* by
**Utagawa Hiroshige.**

Katsushita Hokusai was born in 1760. He was a master of creating woodblock prints. He made pictures by first carving a design into a block of wood. This was dipped into paint and then pressed onto a canvas. He carved a new piece of wood for each color in his pictures.

Utagawa Hiroshige lived in the early 1800s. Like Hokusai, he was a great master of the woodblock print. His works often include beautifully written versions of Japanese poems.

15

Fisherman catch fish in a giant net.

This worker is using technology in an animation studio.

# Jobs

Many Japanese people work with technology. Others work in manufacturing jobs, making everything from cars to computers. Many work for banks, investment firms, stock brokers, and other financial groups. Many others own and run small businesses, such as fish markets and specialty shops.

# Keepsakes

**Netsuke** are tiny, carved figures of people, animals, and objects. They are usually made from wood, bone, or ivory. They were originally used to attach small purses to a kimono's obi. In English, netsuke means "root for fastening." This might be because the first netsuke were made from roots. Very old and expensive netsuke are kept in museums. Modern ones are easy to find and cost much less.

Try these handheld Japanese drums too!

This netsuke is made of ivory.

**Handheld Japanese drum**

# Land

Japan is a nation of islands. There are many seashores, hills, mountains, and volcanoes.

Mount Fuji is Japan's tallest mountain. It is also a volcano! It last erupted in 1707.

Japan is made up of four large islands and hundreds of small ones. In the north, the island of Hokkaido has a wintry climate for part of the year. About 1,000 miles (1,600 km) to the south is the island of Kyushu. There the temperature stays much warmer year-round. Honshu is between them. It is Japan's largest and most populated island. The island of Shikoku sits off its southeastern shore.

Japan is separated from the rest of the Asian continent by water.

## Shima

*(SHE-ma)*
means island.

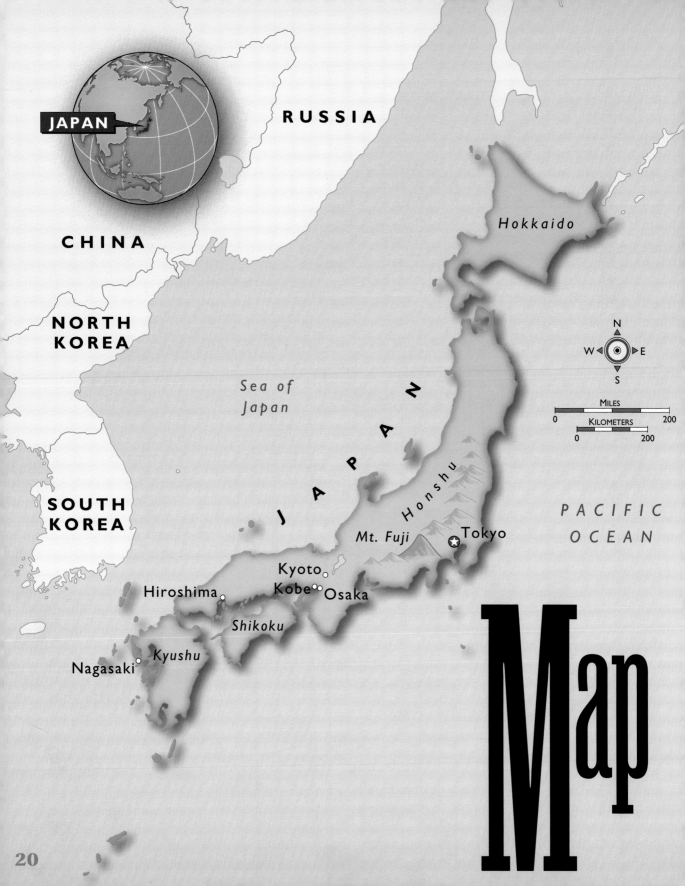

RUSSIA

CHINA

NORTH
KOREA

SOUTH
KOREA

*Hokkaido*

*Sea of
Japan*

N
W ◀ ◉ ▶ E
S

MILES
0 ─────────── 200
KILOMETERS
0 ─────────── 200

J
A
P
A
N

*Honshu*

Mt. Fuji ★ Tokyo

PACIFIC
OCEAN

Kyoto
Kobe
Hiroshima      Osaka

*Shikoku*

Nagasaki  *Kyushu*

Map

# Nation

The Japanese flag has a white background with a large red circle in the middle. The red circle is a symbol of the sun. Japan is sometimes called "the land of the rising sun." The Japanese word for the country is **Nippon**. This word means "the place from which the sun comes." People once believed that the first Japanese emperor was a child of the sun goddess.

# Only in Japan

Visit Japan and you can discover **Bunraku**, **Noh**, and **Kabuki dramas**. These are styles of drama or plays that are performed in front of many fans.

**Kabuki actors use lots of makeup.**

Bunraku is a style of Japanese drama that uses large puppets instead of actors. They make the puppets move in ways that are very lifelike.

Kabuki dramas are full of action. During a Kabuki play, audience members may shout things out to the actors. A Kabuki play lasts for several hours.

Noh dramas are the oldest form of theater in Japan. Performers in Noh plays wear masks. They use a singsong way of speaking to tell the story.

**Actors in Kabuki plays wear bold, colorful costumes.**

23

# People

Belonging to a group is very important to the Japanese. People learn rules for getting along well in their families, with their school friends, and at work.

Japanese homes have everything a family needs, but usually not a lot of furniture.

This Japanese family lives and works on a farm.

The typical Japanese family has only one or two children. Mothers take care of the home, the children, and the family's money. Fathers are responsible for earning the family's money. They often travel long distances to get to work.

Japanese homes have always been small. Today, many people live in apartment buildings. Beds that can be rolled up during the daytime allow families to have extra space.

# Kazoku

*(KA-zoo-koo)*
means family.

25

Karaoke is very popular in Japan.

# Question What is your kakushi gei?

Do you have a good singing voice? Can you play a musical instrument? Are you great at telling jokes or acting in plays? Any of these things might be your kakushi gei. Kakushi gei is a term that means "hidden talent." The Japanese feel it is important for every person to develop a talent. However, they do not think it is polite to brag. Keep your talent a secret until it is your turn to shine!

Statues of the Buddha are found in or near most temples.

The Heian Shrine near Kyoto is famous for its beautiful gardens.

# Religion

**Buddhism** was introduced to Japan from China and Korea. Buddhists believe that a person's life can be made better if he or she focuses on the things that matter most.

**Shinto** is another religion developed in Japan many centuries ago. Followers of the Shinto faith have a deep respect for the natural world. When visiting a Shinto shrine, people will often wash their hands and mouths. They will leave coins or food. Then they will get the attention of the shrine's god by clapping their hands.

27

# School & Sports

In Japan the school year begins in April. Students attend classes from Monday through Friday. Older students attend courses at night to help them study for important tests. Everything about a young person's future is determined by how well he or she does in school.

Japanese sports fans enjoy both watching and playing baseball. Like the United States, Japan has two professional baseball leagues. Martial arts such as judo, karate, and **kendo** are also popular. Sumo wrestling is Japan's most-watched sport.

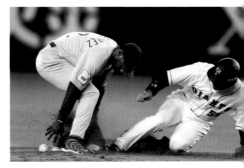

An exciting moment during a game between the Chicago Cubs and the Yomiuri Giants

A bullet train is so fast, it can travel at a speed of nearly 200 miles per hour (320 km per hour).

# Transportation

Japan is famous for being the home of the Shinkansen, or "bullet train." It began running in 1964. It was a symbol to the rest of the world that Japan had become a modern, powerful nation. If your train leaves the station without you, don't worry. Another will be along in just a few minutes. Today, there are many bullet trains in Japan.

A torii marks the entrance to the Itsukushima Shrine.

# Unusual Places

The island of Miyajima is home to one of Japan's most well known landmarks. You can see the famous "floating" shrine there. But, it is not completely true to say that it is a shrine that floats. The shrine is built on an area of land that floods each day as the tide comes in. When it is surrounded by water, the shrine looks as if it is floating on the surface. Its real name is the Itsukushima Shrine.

# Sakura no hana

*(SA-koo-ra no HA-na)*
means cherry blossom.

# Visiting the Country

**A cherry tree blossoms near the Nagoya Castle.**

Cherry trees bloom for less than one week each year. When this happens, the Japanese enjoy gathering under them for outdoor celebrations. Cherry trees are usually planted in long rows or in thick orchards that have hundreds of trees.

The Japanese believe that the blossoms of the cherry tree are more than a symbol of the coming of spring. They are also a reminder that life is beautiful and that beautiful things are often gone too soon.

31

# Window to the Past

In 1945, most of the world was at war. The United States and Japan had been fighting each other for four years.

Today, the ruins of the museum are called the Atomic Bomb Dome. Floating lanterns are symbols of the people who were killed in the explosion.

With each passing month, the United States came closer to winning the war against Japan. However, Japan's government refused to give up. Finally, to bring the war with Japan to an end, the United States dropped **atomic bombs** on the cities of Hiroshima and Nagasaki. Shortly after, Japan agreed to stop fighting. The bombs killed tens of thousands of people instantly. Many more died later.

# X-tra Special Things

Have you ever wished that you could talk to animals?

A long time ago, samarai made swords.

Hotels with tiny, cube-shaped rooms are called "capsule hotels."

Sumo wrestlers square off

In Japan, a machine has been invented that will tell you if your cat's meow is a happy one or a hungry one. It is called the "Meow-Lingual."

Some of the best things in Japan are not new at all. there are **bonsai** trees, sword-making, and sumo wrestling. They have been around for a long time. Bonsai is a way of growing trees so that they remain as small as house plants. Bonsai is a highly respected form of art. In the days of the samurai, sword-making was also a respected craft. Beautiful samurai swords can be seen today in museums.

**Lanterns and parades are features of many of Japan's yearly festivals.**

Costumes are worn by children at rice-planting festivals.

# Yearly Festivals

Many kinds of festivals are celebrated in Japan. There are huge lanterns, colorful parades, and great music.

Ice carvings and fun in the snow at Sapporo's Winter Festival

Children join in many different kinds of festivals. There is the rice-planting festival, the Tsukuba Festival where you can hear great drummers, and the Winter Festival that has a huge playground carved out of ice!

Children also have holidays set aside especially for them. Girls' Day is observed on March 3. It is also known as the Doll Festival. Boys are honored on Children's Day on May 5. On this day, wind socks shaped like **carp** are flown from long poles or above homes. They symbolize strength and courage.

Tsukuba Festival drum

37

Zen gardens can be found near Buddhist shrines or temples. Zen gardens are quiet, peaceful places.

# Zen

**Zen** is one form of the Buddhist religion. Buddhism was practiced in Japan for hundreds of years before Zen became popular. Zen Buddhists try to live simple, quiet lives. They concentrate on hard work. They try not to spend time thinking about getting material things, or holding onto things, or ways in which people might hurt them. This helps them feel at peace on the inside and with the world around them.

## Japanese and English Words

**atomic bomb** a powerful bomb used to destroy entire cities

**bonsai** (BON-sye) the art of growing small trees that are trained into artistic shapes

**Buddhism** a religion based on the teachings of the Buddha

**Bunraku** Japanese puppet theater

**carp** a type of fish often depicted in Japanese paintings

**cicadas** cricketlike insects

**citizen** (SIT-i-zuhn) people who live in a city or town

**constitutional monarchy** a form of government in which power is shared between an emperor (or king or queen), and lawmakers elected by the people

**drama** a type of play

**extinct** no longer alive

**geta** wooden, sandal-like footwear

**Kabuki** a type of Japanese theater known for its elaborate costumes

**kakushi gei** a Japanese phrase that means "hidden talent"

**karaoke** (kah-ree-OH-kee) the art of singing along with prerecorded music

**kendo** a form of martial arts in which opponents fight with bamboo poles

**kimono** a robelike piece of clothing

**macaque** a species of large, furry monkey

**miso soup** a thin, clear soup made from fermented soy bean paste

**netsuke** small, carved figures of animals, people, and objects

**Nippon** the Japanese name for Japan

**Noh** a form of Japanese drama usually about making moral choices

**obi** (OH-bee) the decorative belt or sash worn with a kimono

**samurai** (SAM-oo-rye) Japanese warrior

**Shinto** a religion practiced in Japan

**shogun** a military leader

**shrine** Shinto holy place; a holy building that often contains sacred objects

**tabi** women's ankle-length white socks worn with a kimono

**temple** Buddhist holy place; a building used for worship

**torii** carved post with a crossbeam that marks the entrance to a Shinto shrine

**warrior** (WOR-ee-ur) a soldier, or someone who fights in battles

**Zen** a way of thinking that is associated with the Buddhist religion

## Let's Explore More

**Cooking the Japanese Way** by Reiko Weston, Lerner Publications, 2002

**Japan** by Ann Heinrichs, Children's Press, 1997

**Look What Came from Japan** by Miles Harvey, Franklin Watts, 1999

### Websites

**http://www.jinjapan.org**
At this site sponsored by the Japan Information Network, learn more about all things Japanese. Includes instructions for Japanese art forms like *origami* (paper-folding), *ikebana* (flower-arranging), *shado* (calligraphy), and many more.

**http://www.pitt.edu/~dash/japan.html**
Visit this site to read some Japanese folk tales.

*Italic* page numbers indicate illustrations.

# Meet the Author

**JEFF REYNOLDS** was raised on a farm in Illinois. He has lived in Minneapolis-St. Paul, New York City, and Connecticut, and now lives and works in Washington, D.C. He received a B.A. from Western Illinois University and an M.A. in Theater History and Criticism from Brooklyn College. At various times he has been a farmer, milk man, school custodian, housepainter, hotel bellman, stamp dealer, teacher, librarian, actor, journalist, and editor. He is also the author of *A to Z books* about Germany, Japan, Puerto Rico, and United States of America.